Table of Contents

Vintage Kitchen Cover-Up, page 4

Apron Elegance, page 36

Very Berry, page 44

Basic Sewing Supplies & Equipment

- Hand-sewing needles and thimble
- Marking pens or tailor's chalk
- Measuring tools: tape measure and ruler
- Pattern tracing paper or cloth
- Point turner
- Pressing tools: ham and tailor's boards
- Pressing equipment: board and iron, and press cloths
- Rotary cutter, mats and straightedges
- Scissors
- Sewing machine and matching thread
- Serger, if desired
- Straight pins and pincushion
- Spray adhesive (temporary)
- Seam sealant
- Seam ripper

House of White Birches, Berne, Indiana 46711   DRGnetwork.com

Vintage Kitchen Cover-Up

By Missy Shepler

An heirloom handkerchief adds an extra touch of tenderness to this ruffled apron remake.

Finished Size
Adult large

Finished Measurements
Overall length, excluding adjustable
neck strap: 32 inches
Waist, excluding ties: 39 inches

Materials
- 42-inch-wide lightweight woven fabric:
    1½ yards floral print
    1 yard coordinating tonal print
- Handkerchief, at least 10½ inches across diagonal
- 4 or more buttons
- 6-strand embroidery floss
- Basic sewing supplies and equipment

Cutting
Enlarge templates (page 7) for apron front/lining, pocket, neck strap and ties as indicated.

From floral print (A):
- Cut one apron front.
- Cut one pocket.
- Cut two neck straps.
- Cut two ties.
- Cut three 3½-inch strips the width of the fabric for ruffle.

From coordinating tonal print (B):
- Cut one apron lining.
- Cut one pocket.
- Cut two neck straps.
- Cut two ties.
- Cut three 3½-inch strips the width of the fabric for ruffle.

6

Assembly

Use ¼-inch seam allowance unless otherwise indicated. Sew right sides together.

1. Sew one (A) tie and one (B) tie right sides together, leaving short non-angled end open for turning. Clip corners and turn right side out. Press. Repeat for second tie.

2. Sew one (A) neck strap and one (B) neck strap right sides together, leaving short straight end open for turning. Clip curves and turn right side out. Press. Repeat for second neck strap.

3. Sew short ends of ruffle strips right sides together to form one long strip. Press seam allowances open. Fold strip in half lengthwise, right sides together, and press. Measure 105-inches from short end. Mark and clip excess tie. Sew both short ends and one long edge. Clip corners and turn to right side. Press. Stitch three gathering threads along the unstitched edge of ruffle. Evenly gather ruffle to 73 inches.

4. Sew one (A) pocket and one (B) pocket right sides together along outer edge, leaving a 2-inch opening for turning. Clip corners and turn right side out, turning under unstitched seam allowance of opening. Press. Hand-stitch opening closed. Turn down one upper pocket corner, forming a thin triangle at upper pocket edge. Use embroidery floss to stitch a button on pocket corner to hold triangular edge in place.

5. Press handkerchief in half diagonally with right sides together. Place (B) apron right side up on work surface. Center folded handkerchief wrong side up on top of apron (B), matching pressed fold with apron front neck edge.

6. Using neck strap placement pattern markings as a guide, snip two slits in folded handkerchief edge. Insert neck straps through slits between handkerchief layers so raw edges are matching and (A) sides of ties are toward (B) side of apron (Figure 1).

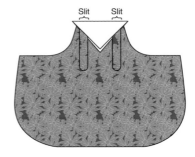

Figure 1

7. Place (A) apron over (B) apron with right sides together, aligning upper edges. Pin through all layers, being careful not to catch extended neck straps or lower edge of handkerchief in seam areas. Sew top apron neck together. Press.

Note: *If handkerchief extends past upper edge of apron, fold corners to form a pleat and pin excess handkerchief away from seam line while stitching (Figure 2).*

Figure 2

8. Pin short, unstitched ends of apron ties between aprons at tie placement leaving ¼ inch above tie for armsyce seam (Figure 3). With right sides together, pin ruffle between aprons, beginning and ending just below ties. Adjust ruffles evenly. Sew lower portion of apron together. Trim corners and clip curves. Turn right side out. Press, turning under seam allowance of opening. Hand-stitch opening closed.

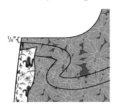

Figure 3

9. Sew along armsyce edges of apron, pivoting at corners (Figure 4). On one side, leave a 6-inch opening for turning. Clip corners, press seam open. Turn apron to right side. Hand-stitch opening closed to finish.

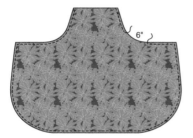

Figure 4

10. Overlap neck straps and tack in place with buttons and embroidery floss. ❖

Don't Cut It!

If slicing into an heirloom goes against your grain, alter the neck straps so you don't have to cut the handkerchief.

1. Fold handkerchief right sides together and sandwich between apron pieces, aligning folded edge with neckline edge. Stitch along the seam line.

2. Lengthen neck straps, if needed, and sew short straight edges together to make two long straps.

3. Place straps right sides together and sew around outer edges, leaving an opening for turning. Turn and press. Hand-stitch opening closed.

4. Tack strap ends to apron with buttons.

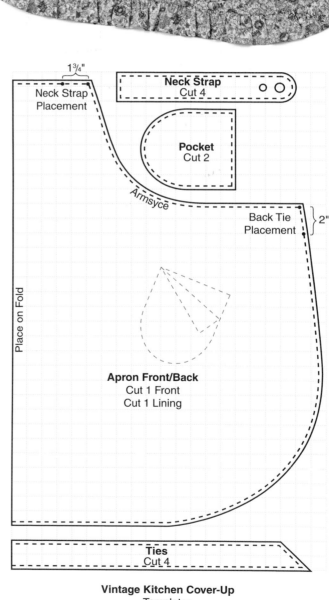

Vintage Kitchen Cover-Up
Templates
1 square = 1"

Something to Crow About

By Chris Malone

Greet the new day with a cock-a-doodle-do when you wear this rooster-inspired creation.

Finished Size
Adult medium

Finished Measurements
Overall length, excluding nonadjustable neck strap: 39 inches
Length to waist: 11 inches
Width at waist: 17 inches

Materials
- 44/45-inch-wide lightweight woven fabric:
  - 1⅞ yards multicolored print
  - ⅔ yard coordinating stripe
  - ⅞ yard contrasting print
- 2 (⅞-inch) buttons to match pocket
- No. 8–12 pearl cotton or similar thin cord
- Basic sewing supplies and equipment

Cutting
From multicolored print:
- Cut two 40 x 24-inch rectangles for skirt.
- Cut two 12 x 12-inch squares for bib.

From coordinating stripe:
- Cut three 5 x 40-inch strips for ruffle.
- Cut two 6½ x 24-inch strips for neck strap.

From contrasting print:
- Cut two 18 x 3-inch strips for waistband and lining.
- Cut two 6½ x 30-inch strips for ties.
- Cut two 6 x 6-inch squares for pocket.

Assembly
Use ½-inch seam allowance unless otherwise indicated. Sew right sides together.

1. Fold one skirt rectangle in half to measure 20 x 24 inches. Mark 8 inches from bottom on open side and draw a line from this point to bottom edge at fold (Figure 1). Cut on line to form V shape. Repeat with second skirt rectangle.

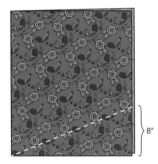

8"

Figure 1

2. Join ruffle strips at short ends to make one strip 5 x 118 inches. Trim seams to ¼ inch and press open. Press a double ¼-inch hem on one long edge and both short edges. Topstitch in place.

3. Gather upper edge of ruffle ½ inch from raw edge by stitching with an open zigzag over pearl cotton (Figure 2), beginning and ending ½ inch from each end. Before pulling on pearl cotton to gather, divide and mark ruffle into quarters. Repeat for bottom edge of skirt with center at bottom point and ends ½ inch from each side (Figure 3 on page 10). Pull cord to gather ruffle to fit bottom of skirt. Pin ruffle to skirt, matching quarter marks. Adjust gathers evenly between quarter marks and sew in place.

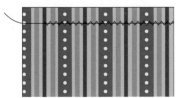

Figure 2

Figure 3

4. With right sides together, sew skirt pieces together along side and bottom edges with ruffle sandwiched between. Grade seam allowance. Turn right side out and press. Topstitch ¼ inch from side and bottom seams.

5. Gather top edge of skirt using cord and zigzag stitch, sewing through both layers. Pull cord to gather top of skirt to 17 inches wide. Pin gathered skirt to one waistband, right sides together, with seam allowance extended on each end of waistband. Adjust gathers evenly. Sew in place (Figure 4).

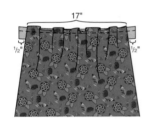

Figure 4   **Figure 5**

6. Fold strap in half lengthwise, right sides together, and sew along long edge, leaving ends open. Press seam, turn right side out and repress. Adjust length of strap, trimming ends as needed. Fold a small pleat in the narrow end of each strap end so end width is 2 inches. Machine-baste pleat into place. Pin strap ends to bib top edge, matching raw edges, with each strap end ½ inch from corners. Sew in place (Figure 5).

7. With right sides together, sew bib front and lining together across sides and top edges, sandwiching strap between. Grade seam allowance and trim corners. Turn right side out and press. Center and pin bottom edge of bib front to remaining long edge of waistband on skirt, right sides together. Sew in place (Figure 6).

Figure 6

8. Fold ties in half lengthwise with right sides together. Sew along long edge and one end. Trim corners. Turn right side out and press. Fold a small pleat in the center of each unstitched end so it measures 1⅞ inches wide. Machine-baste to hold.

9. Place pleated end of each tie on waistband front with raw edges even (Figure 7). Baste in place.

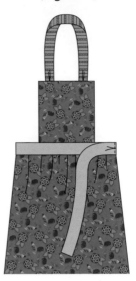

Figure 7

10. Press under ½ inch on one long edge of remaining waistband. Place waistbands right sides together with ends of ties sandwiched between and folded edges of waistband at bottom. Sew across side and top edges (Figure 8). Turn right side out. Press. Hand-stitch folded edge in place.

Figure 8

11. Pin pocket squares with right sides together. Sew around, leaving a 2-inch opening on one side. Trim corners. Turn right side out. Fold in seam allowance on opening and press. Pin pocket to skirt front at a 45-degree angle, 4 inches from waistband and 8 inches from side. Topstitch close to side and bottom edges. Sew a button to each top corner of pocket. ❖

Source: *Possibilities—Café Euopa fabric collection from Quilting Treasures.*

Pop-Over Smock

By Janis Bullis

This vintage-style inspired smock is the perfect expression for your creativity.

Finished Size
Adult medium/large

Finished Measurements
Length from shoulders: 37 inches

Materials
- 44/45-inch-wide lightweight woven fabric:
    1½ yards plum/cream stripe
    ⅜ yard coordinating plum print (A)
    ⅜ yard coordinating solid-color
    1 yard coordinating plum print (B)
- ⅓ yard lightweight fusible interfacing
- 2 buttons
- Basic sewing supplies and equipment

Cutting
Enlarge templates for apron front, apron back and pocket (page 12) as indicated.

From stripe fabric:
- Cut one apron front on fold.
- Cut two apron backs.

From coordinating print (A) fabric:
- Cut two pockets.

From solid-color fabric:
- Cut two pockets.

From coordinating print (B) fabric:
- Cut 2½-inch bias strips to equal 5 yards when joined, for binding.

From fusible interfacing:
- Cut two pockets.

Assembly
Use ½-inch seam allowance unless otherwise indicated. Sew right sides together.

1. Sew apron front and back at side seams. Allow back sections to criss-cross naturally and sew front to back at shoulder seams (Figure 1).

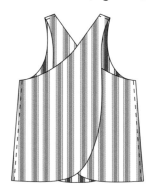

Figure 1

2. Measure and mark the ½-inch stitching line at the point of both V shapes along the scalloped hemline. To reinforce, stitch along marked line (Figure 2). Clip seam allowance to, but not through, stitching.

Figure 2

House of White Birches, Berne, Indiana 46711   DRGnetwork.com

3. Sew together short ends of three binding strips to make one long strip. Trim seams and press open. With wrong sides together, press strip in half lengthwise. Sew and press remaining three binding strips in same manner. Mark center of each binding strip.

4. Begin pinning first strip to bottom front of apron, matching centers, with raw edges even. Stitch to each V in the scallop on the front. Continue pinning binding to hemline and up the back of the apron, stopping 5 inches from ends of the strip.

5. Pin second binding strip to neckline front, matching centers, and pinning over shoulders and around underarms, then up over the shoulder again until the tail ends are near end of the first strip.

6. Pin and sew ends of strips, removing excess fabric from binding as needed. Pin remaining unsewn strip to apron. Stitch and press seam allowances toward binding. Fold binding over seam allowance to wrong side and pin folded edge along stitching line. Slip-stitch or baste in place, folding a mitered tuck in binding at scallop points.

7. On right side, topstitch close to seam along entire edge of binding.

8. Apply interfacing to wrong side of each solid-color pocket. With right sides together, pin solid-color and print pocket pieces together and sew around edges, leaving an opening for turning. Trim seam to ⅛ inch. Turn right side out. Press, turning under seam allowance on opening. Slip-stitch opening closed. Press pocket flat. Topstitch around edges.

9. Position pockets on apron front, turning down a 2¾-inch top flap. Top stitch lower edge of pocket to secure to apron. ❖

Source: Sophia fabric collection from Quilting Treasures.

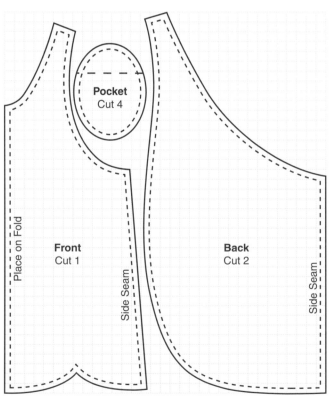

Place on Fold

Front Cut 1

Side Seam

Pocket Cut 4

Back Cut 2

Side Seam

Pop-Over Smock
Templates
1 square = 1"

Sassy Pink Floral Apron

By Phyllis Dobbs

Creativity is easy when you start with your heart in this heart-shaped bodice full-length apron.

Finished Size
Adult medium

Finished Measurements
Overall length, excluding adjustable neck straps: 33 inches
Length to waist: 11 inches
Width at waist: 20 inches

Materials
- 44/45-inch-wide lightweight woven fabric:
    1⅔ yards pink floral
    ⅝ yards green tonal
- ¾-inch yellow shank button
- Basic sewing supplies and equipment

Cutting
Enlarge templates (page 16) for apron bodice/bodice facing and pocket as indicated.

From pink floral fabric:
- Cut one 56 x 21-inch rectangle for apron skirt.
- Cut one apron bodice on fold.
- Cut one bodice lining on fold.

From green tonal fabric:
- Cut 4 pockets.
- Cut two 2½ x 19-inch strips for neck straps.
- Cut four 3½-inch strips the width of the fabric for ties.

Assembly
Use ½-inch seam allowance unless otherwise indicated. Sew right sides together.

1. Fold each 2½ x 19-inch strip for neck tie in half lengthwise, with wrong sides together. Sew one short end, and continue across long edge leaving remaining end open for turning. Turn right side out and press.

2. With right sides together, sew short ends of two 3½-inch strips for ties to form an 88-inch-long strip. Press seam open. Repeat for second tie.

3. With right sides together, sew two pockets together on the sides and bottom. Clip corners, press seams open and turn. Fold top edges ⅝ inch to inside, press. Sew across the top of the pocket ¼ inch from the top folded edge, using a decorative stitch, if desired. Repeat for second pocket.

4. Pin raw edge of neck straps on right side of bodice (Figure 1). Place lining with wrong side up on stack. Pin, and stitch, catching ends of straps in seam. Clip the center point. Press seam allowances and turn bodice to right side. Press. Topstitch side and upper edge.

Figure 1

5. Sew a gathering stitch 3 inches on each side of bodice center point. Pull gathers tight and topstitch to hold in place. Hand-stitch button at the center point.

6. Turn and press a ¼-inch double hem around the side and bottom edges of apron skirt. Topstitch into place. Pin pockets 13½ inches from each side and 9 inches above the bottom. Topstitch pockets to apron body.

7. Fold bodice in half lengthwise and mark center of bottom edge. Fold and mark the center of one waist tie in the same manner. With right sides together,

and matching the center points, pin the tie on top of the bodice, overlapping the bottom edge of the bodice by ½ inch. Sew into place (Figure 2).

the apron to opposite tie edge of bodice, matching centers (Figure 3). Stitch.

Figure 2

Figure 3

8. Mark the center of the skirt. Stitch two gathering threads along the top edge. Gather skirt to 19 inches. With right sides together, pin the gathered edge of

Figure 4

9. Sew long ends of tie together, press and turn to right side. Press under raw edge of tie at bodice and apron (Figure 4). Topstitch the tie to the apron bodice and skirt, continuing stitching around ends of ties. ❖

Source: *The Pink Ribbon Companions II and Prism fabric from Quilting Treasures.*

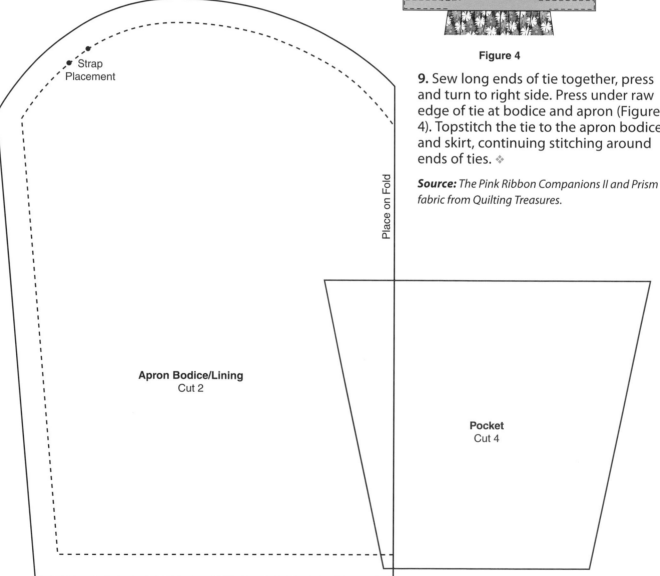

Strap
Placement

Place on Fold

Apron Bodice/Lining
Cut 2

Pocket
Cut 4

Sassy Pink Floral Apron
Templates
Enlarge 200%

Chocolate Lover's Apron

By Connie Kauffman

Combine chocolate with sewing and you'll have a winning combination for kitchen wear.

Finished Size
Adult small (medium/large) (extra-large)

Instructions/measurements are given for size small, with those for larger sizes in parentheses. When only one reference is given, it applies to all sizes.

Finished Measurements
Overall length, excluding adjustable neck straps: 27½ (30) (32) inches
Length to waist: 7⅞ (9) (10) inches
Width at waist: 15½ (20) (25) inches

Materials
- 3 coordinating prints 44/45-inch-wide lightweight woven fabric:
    ¼ (⅓) (⅓) yard print for bodice
    ½ yard print for skirt
    ½ (⅝) (⅝) yard print for remaining pieces
- Basic sewing supplies and equipment

Cutting
From print for bodice:
• Cut two 8 x 8 (9 x 10) (10 x 12)-inch pieces.

From print for skirt:
• Cut one 18 x 24 (18 x 26) (18 x 32)-inch piece.

From print for remaining pieces:
• Cut two 16½ x 3 (19½ x 3) (22½ x 3)-inch strips for waistband.
• Cut two 3-inch strips the width of the fabric for ties.
• Cut two 2-inch strips the width of the fabric for neck straps and binding.

House of White Birches, Berne, Indiana 46711   DRGnetwork.com

Assembly

Use ¼-inch seam allowance unless otherwise indicated. Sew right sides together.

1. Press each 2-inch strip for neck straps and binding in half lengthwise with wrong sides together. Open strip and press long edges to center crease, then fold and press again on first crease.

2. Place two bodice pieces wrong sides together, matching raw edges. Cover top raw edge of bodice pieces with a length of neck strap/binding and topstitch, catching folded edges of binding on both sides of bodice (Figure 1).

Figure 1

3. Cut remaining strip in half. Topstitch to sides of bodice, turning ends in (Figure 2).

Figure 2

4. Turn under a double ¼-inch hem on sides and bottom of skirt. Topstitch in place. Gather top raw edge of skirt to 16½ (19½) (22½) inches. Sew gathered edge of skirt to one waistband strip between seam allowances on each end (Figure 3). Press seam toward waistband.

16½ (19½) (22½)"

Figure 3

5. Center bodice over top of same waistband strip (Figure 4). Place second waistband strip over bodice, right side down. Sew through all three layers. Press waistband down.

Figure 4

6. Fold each tie strip right sides together. Beginning 3 inches from short end, sew each long edge, tapering off to a point before stitching remaining long edge (Figure 5).

3"

Figure 5

7. With right sides together, sew end of each tie to end of waistband (Figure 6). Press seam.

Figure 6

8. Press under seam allowance in tie opening and slipstitch closed. Turn under seam allowance on bottom edge of back waistband and hand-stitch in place. Hand-tack waistband to bib along sides. ❖

Source: *Fabric from Moda Fabrics.*

Handy Helper

By Missy Shepler

Daily chores don't need to be dull. This fun and functional apron takes the tedium out of everyday tasks.

Finished Size
Adult medium

Finished Measurements
Length from shoulders: 30½ inches
Length to waist: 15 inches
Waist, excluding ties: 30 inches

Materials
- 42-inch-wide lightweight woven fabric:
    1 yard large floral print (A)
    1½ yards coordinating small floral print (B)
    1 panel of fabric for front pocket (or ½ yard of print) (C)
- 3 buttons
- Basic sewing supplies and equipment

Cutting
Enlarge templates (page 23) for apron skirt front/lining, bib front/lining, bib back/lining and bib pocket as indicated.

From large floral print (A):
- Cut one apron skirt for lining.
- Cut two bib backs, reversing one.
- Cut one bib front.
- Cut two 2 x 40-inch strips for ties.

From coordinating small floral print (B):
- Cut one apron skirt for front.
- Cut two bib backs for lining, reversing one.
- Cut one front pocket for lining.
- Cut one bib pocket for lining.
- Cut one bib front.

From panel fabric (C):
- Cut one front pocket.
- Cut one bib pocket.
- Cut two 2 x 40-inch strips for ties.

Assembly
Use ¼-inch seam allowance unless otherwise indicated. Sew right sides together.

1. Sew (B) and (C) bib pocket together, leaving a 2-inch opening for turning. Clip curves and turn right side out. Press, turning under seam allowance of opening. Hand-stitch opening closed.

2. Adjust shoulder straps on bib front and back as needed. Sew bib front and back (A) together at shoulders with right sides together. Press seams open. Repeat with bib front and back for lining (B). With raw edges even and right sides together, sew bibs together along neck and curved back openings. Repeat to sew armsyce. (Figure 1). Clip curves. Trim seam allowance. Press. Turn bib to the right side by flipping front bib inside out and pulling back bodice through front opening.

Figure 1

3. Position bib pocket on front bib. Pin into place. Topstitch side and bottom edges. Topstitch bib around inner and outer edges close to edge. *Note: Do not stitch into waist seam allowance.*

4. Sew (B) and (C) front pockets together along pocket edges only. Clip curves. Turn right side out. Press. Topstitch pocket edges, ending stitching at seam lines to complete front pocket unit (Figure 2).

Figure 2

5. Place skirt front (B) with right side up. Place completed pocket unit over it with (C) on top (Figure 3). Complete sandwich by placing skirt front (C) with wrong side up. Sew all layers together leaving pocket area open. Clip curves. Turn right side out. Press.

Figure 3

6. Topstitch lower edge of panel to skirt front. Stay stitch top waist edges of skirt front and panel.

7. Press under ¼ inch on bottom edges of bib front and back lining (B). With front (A) sides together, sew bib front to skirt, matching centers. ***Note:*** *Take care not to catch pressed edge of lining in stitching.*

8. With front (A) sides together, match (*) on skirt front with (*) on bib back. Sew from each (*) to curved back openings. Press seams toward bib backs. Machine- or hand-stitch pressed edges of bib linings over seams.

9. Sew short ends of ties (B) and (C) together to make one 80-inch-long strip of each fabric. Mark short ends of (B) at a 45-degree angle. Sew (B) and (C) strips together along two short angled ends and one long side. Trim angled ends, clip corners and grade seam allowances.

10. On wrong side, press long seam, pushing seam allowance toward darker fabric. Turn to right side. Press seam allowance to wrong side on long unfinished edges.

11. Center tie along apron waistline, aligning top (stitched) edges of tie over waistline seam. Pin. Topstitch tie to apron waistline, continuing stitching around ties to finish.

12. Overlap back edges, leaving a keyhole opening at back waist where ties meet. Tack back edges together with a button. Sew remaining two buttons at shoulders. ❖

Source: *In My Garden fabric collection from Quilting Treasures.*

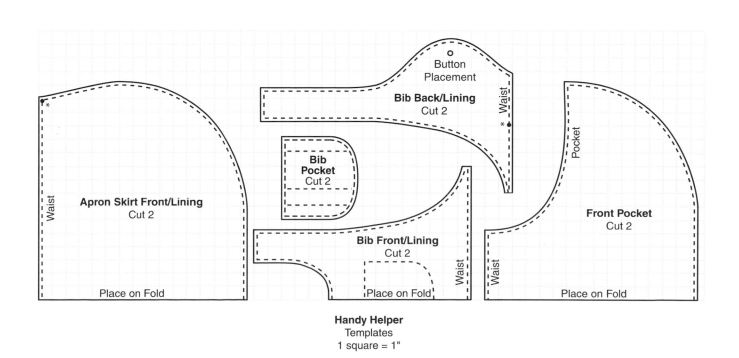

Handy Helper
Templates
1 square = 1"

Gingerbread Men Apron

By Janice Loewenthal

Sweetened with dancing gingerbread men, this apron will inspire you to create uncommonly good confectionaries.

Finished Size
Adult medium

Finished Measurements
Length: 23 inches
Width at waist: 18½ inches

Materials
- 44/45-inch-wide lightweight woven fabric:
    1 yard tan/blue print
    1 yard coordinating blue print (A)
    ⅛ yard coordinating blue print (B)
    ¼ yard brown tonal for appliqués
- 1 yard self-adhesive paper-backed fusible web
- 1⅜ yard fabric stabilizer
- Buttons:
    10 (¼-inch) white
    10 (½-inch) brown
- 6-strand off-white embroidery floss
- Basic sewing supplies and equipment

Cutting
From tan/blue print:
- Cut one 44 x 22½-inch rectangle for apron front.
- Cut one 4 x 19-inch strip for waistband.
- Cut two 3½ x 22-inch strips for ties.

From coordinating blue print (A):
- Cut one 44 x 22½-inch rectangle for apron lining.

Note: Coordinating blue print (B) will be used for star appliqués.

From fabric stabilizer:
- Cut one 5 x 44-inch strip for scallops template.

Appliqués
1. Enlarge gingerbread man, heart and star templates (page 26) as indicated. Trace five gingerbread men, five stars and six hearts onto paper side of fusible web. Cut out just outside traced lines.

2. Fuse shapes onto wrong sides of appropriate fabric:
- Gingerbread men—Brown tonal.
- Hearts—Coordinating blue print (A).
- Stars—Coordinating blue print (B).

Scallops Template
Note: *Enlarge templates (page 26) for scallop 1 and scallop 2 as indicated.*

1. Align longer edge of scallop 1 template with corner of 5 x 45-inch strip of fabric stabilizer and trace edge.

2. Turn scallop template 1 over to reverse it. Align with opposite corner of stabilizer strip and trace edge.

3. Position and trace five scallop 2 templates evenly spaced between the two end scallops.

4. Stabilizer may be trimmed away now, or trimmed with fabric when cutting bottom edge of apron.

Assembly
Use ¼-inch seam allowance unless otherwise indicated.

1. Place apron front and lining wrong sides together with edges even. Pin stabilizer scallops template slightly above bottom edge (Figure 1). Trim scallop edge. Separate apron front and lining.

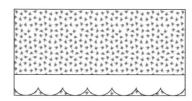

Figure 1

2. Remove paper backing from star appliqués and position on gingerbread men appliqués. Remove backing from gingerbread men appliqués and position on apron front scallops, then remove backing from heart appliqués and position on each side of gingerbread men. Fuse in place.

3. Trace mouth on each gingerbread man. With a piece of stabilizer behind each appliqué, use a backstitch to sew over traced lines and around edges of each appliqué using coordinating threads. Sew on brown buttons for cheeks and white buttons for eyes. Use two strands embroidery floss to embroider eyebrows with straight stitches.

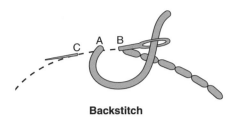

Backstitch

4. Sew apron front and lining, right sides together, around side and bottom edges using a scant ¼-inch seam allowance. Snip curves where scallops come to a point. Turn and press.

5. Gather top edge to 18½ inches, beginning and ending gathering stitches ¼ inch from each edge. Distribute gathers evenly.

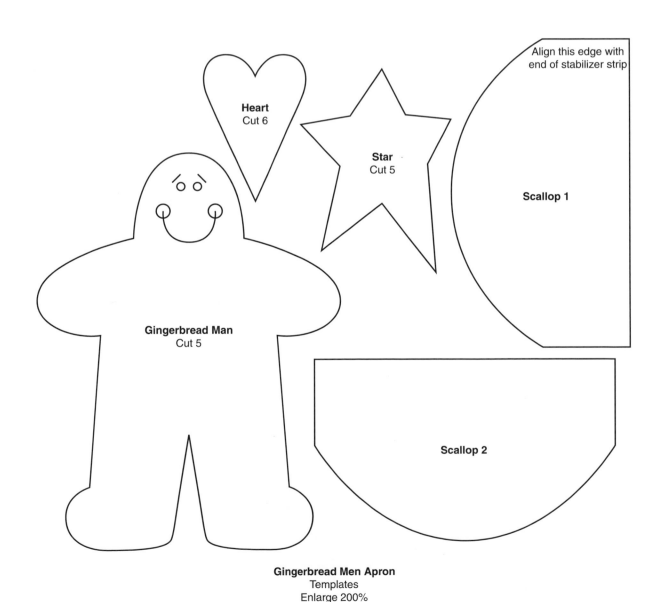

Heart
Cut 6

Star
Cut 5

Align this edge with end of stabilizer strip

Scallop 1

Gingerbread Man
Cut 5

Scallop 2

Gingerbread Men Apron
Templates
Enlarge 200%

6. Press under ¼ inch on one long edge of waist-band; topstitch. Press under ¼ inch on each short edge. Fold waistband in half lengthwise with wrong sides together and press. Open waistband. With right sides together, sew raw long edge of waist-band to gathered edge (Figure 2).

of tie. Turn raw edges on one end of each tie to inside ¼ inch and stitch across.

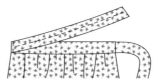

Figure 3

8. Pin raw ends of ties to waistband, seam side facing up, so top edge of tie is even with center crease of waistband. Fold band over (Figure 3). Sew across ends to secure ties. Hand-stitch remaining edge of waistband in place. ❖

Figure 2

7. Fold each tie in half with right sides together and sew down long edge. Turn right side out. Press with seam in center

Source: *Aunt Josie's Log Cabin fabric collection from Quilting Treasures.*

House of White Birches, Berne, Indiana 46711   DRGnetwork.com

Oilcloth Polka Dot

By Carolyn Vagts

Make a durable apron from oilcloth for gardening and heavy-duty jobs, or use the same pattern to create a classy apron for hosting a casual dinner, simply by selecting different fabrics!

Finished Size
Adult medium/large

Finished Measurements
Overall length, excluding nonadjustable neck strap: 26 inches
Length to waist: 14 inches
Width at waist: 26½ inches

Materials
- 1 yard 44/45-inch-wide oilcloth or main fabric for apron front
- 44/45-inch-wide lightweight cotton fabric:
    1½ yards coordinating print
    ⅛ yard contrasting print
- Basic sewing supplies and equipment

Cutting
Enlarge templates (page 31) for apron body, yoke and pocket as indicated.

From oilcloth or main fabric:
• Cut one apron front.

From the coordinating print:
• Cut one apron lining.
• Cut four 3½-inch strips the width of the fabric for neck strap, ties and front lower band.
• Cut one yoke on fold.
• Cut four pockets.

From contrasting print:
• Cut one 1¼-inch strip the width of the fabric for binding.

Assembly
Use ¼-inch seam allowance unless otherwise indicated.

1. Fold each of three 3½-inch strips of coordinating print right sides together and press. Sew the long raw edges together. Turn right side out and press with seam in center. Top stitch ¼ inch from each edge. Set aside for neck strap and ties.

2. Fold the 1¼-inch binding strip in half with wrong sides together. Cut a length of the strip to fit bottom edge of yoke; sew on the right side of yoke piece with raw edges even (Figure 1). Press binding down with seam toward yoke (Figure 2).

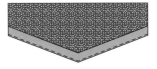

Figure 1

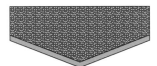

Figure 2

3. Cut a length of the binding strip to fit across the top edge of each pocket with ends extending an inch on each side. Sew binding to tops of two pockets in same manner as for yoke, only start and stop ¼ inch from each end (Figure 3). Fold up the ends in a 90-degree angle and pin (Figure 4). Lay the remaining two pockets on tops of units with right sides together and stitch around, leaving a 2-inch opening for turning (Figure 5). Turn and press.

Figure 3

Figure 4

Figure 5

4. Place yoke on apron front, matching A dots for yoke. Place pockets on apron front, using measurements provided in Figure 6. Topstitch in place ⅛ inch from edges.

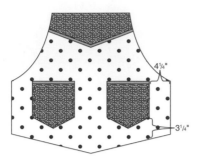

Figure 6

5. Cut the remaining 3½-inch strip in half across the 3½-inch width. Place on one angled side of bottom apron front with right sides together, leaving 2 inches extended at each end. Stitch into place,

stopping ¼ inch from the point (Figure 7). Repeat on opposite angled side.

Figure 7

6. Fold lower bands so folds meet at center, with excess fabric at back (Figure 8); press to crease. Open bands and pin together. Sew on creased line to miter the point, sewing from the point of the apron front to the outer edge (Figure 9). Trim seam allowance to ¼ inch and press open (Figure 10).

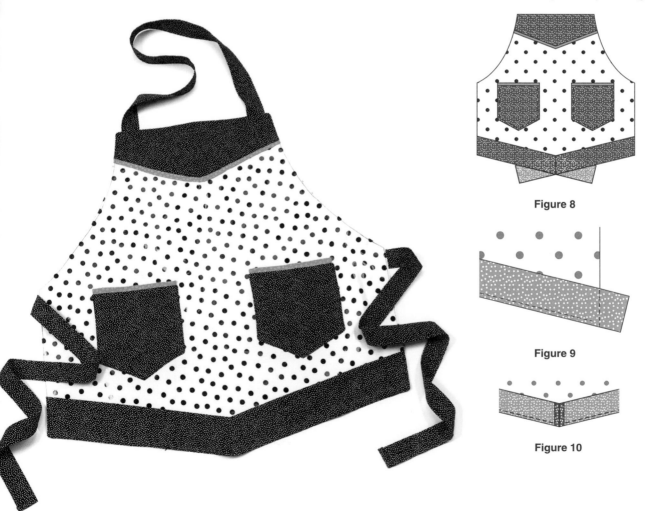

Figure 8

Figure 9

Figure 10

7. Pin neck strap and ties (from step 1) in place (Figure 11). Adjust length of neck strap; trim ends as needed, then repin.

½" ½"
½" ½"

Figure 11

8. Place apron front and lining right sides together, sandwiching neck strap and ties between. Sew around outer edges, leaving an opening in one side for turning (Figure 12). Turn and press. Hand-stitch opening closed.

Figure 12

9. Topstitch ¼ inch from edge. Trim ties to desired lengths, then turn under and stitch to finish ends. ❖

Sources: *Oilcloth from Oilcloth International Inc.; Sahara fabric from Blank Quilting.*

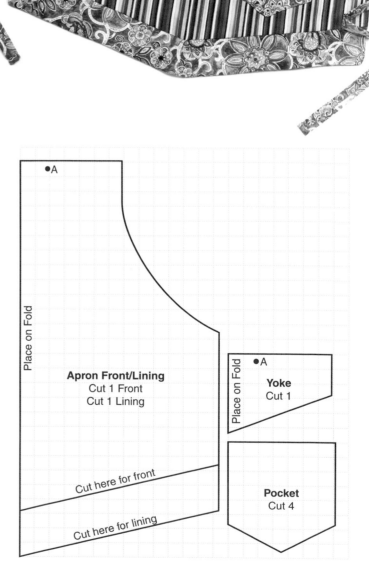

Place on Fold

● A

Apron Front/Lining
Cut 1 Front
Cut 1 Lining

Cut here for front

Cut here for lining

Place on Fold

● A

Yoke
Cut 1

Pocket
Cut 4

Oilcloth Polka Dot
Templates
1 square = 1"

Petals Ahead

By Chris Malone

Complete with a detachable garden flower, you'll love creating perfect petals as a hem accent for this pleasing apron.

Finished Size
Adult small/medium

Finished Measurements
Length, including leaves: 22 inches
Width at waist: 17 inches

Materials
- 44/45-inch-wide lightweight woven fabric:
  ¾ yard green-with-white print
  ¼ yard each 4 coordinating white-with-green prints (A, B, C and D)
- ½ yard light- to medium weight nonwoven interfacing
- Scrap fleece or batting
- 1⅛-inch shank button
- Permanent fabric adhesive
- Optional: pin back
- Basic sewing supplies and equipment

Cutting
From green-with-white print:
- Cut one 41 x 18-inch rectangle for skirt.
- Cut one 40 x 3½-inch strip for hem facing.
- Cut two 6 x 6-inch squares for pocket.

From white-with-green print (A):
- Cut one 18 x 4½-inch strip for waistband.

From white-with-green print (B):
- Cut two 5½ x 30-inch strips for ties.

From white-with-green print (C):
- Cut one 4 x 21-inch strip for flower.

Note: White-with-green print (D) will be used to cut leaves.

Leaves
1. Use template (page 35) to trace leaf 15 times on wrong side of half of white-with-green print (D), leaving ½ inch between each leaf.

2. Fold fabric in half with right sides together, with traced pattern on top. Pin to interfacing. Stitch on outer traced lines, leaving bottom edges open.

3. Cut out ⅛ inch from stitching. Trim interfacing close to seam and trim tips. Turn right side out. Press.

4. Use soluble marking pen to transfer vein lines to one side of each leaf. Stitch on lines with contrasting thread by beginning at leaf base and stitching up to the tip, then rotating and stitching down to the first V. Stitch each line twice as you return to the base (Figure 1).

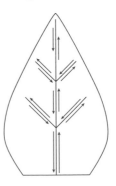

Figure 1

Assembly
Use ½-inch seam allowance unless otherwise indicated. Sew right sides together.

1. Fold and press under ½ inch on both 41-inch sides of skirt. Repeat ½ inch fold for a 1-inch double hem. Press.

2. Unfold pressed side hems. Arrange 13 leaves across bottom of skirt with right sides together and raw edges even, leaving approximately ½ inch between leaves at their widest point with tips pointing to the top of the apron. (Figure 2). Position beginning and end leaf 1½ inches from side hem. Machine-baste in place.

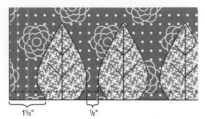

Figure 2

3. Fold and press a ½-inch hem along one long edge of the hem facing. Pin unpressed side of facing to skirt bottom, right sides together, with leaves between. Sew side and bottom edges. Trim corners and grade seams. Turn facing to right side and press. Turning the facing will also turn the side hems on the skirt another ½ inch; press.

4. Topstitch along bottom of skirt ¼ inch from seam. Stitch facing hem close to fold. Stitch side hems.

5. Gather top edge of skirt to 17 inches. Sew skirt to waistband, right sides together, leaving seam allowances extended on waistband (Figure 3). Press under ½ inch on opposite long edge of waistband.

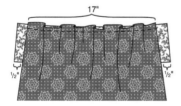

Figure 3

Tips & Techniques

Attaching an embellishment with a pin back allows it to be removed for washing, or for use on other clothing or accessory items. Try accenting your flower creations with buttons or machine embroidery for interest.

6. Fold each tie in half lengthwise, right sides together, and sew across long edge and one short end. Trim corners and turn right side out. Press. Pin raw ends of ties to ends of waistband (Figure 4). Machine-baste to hold.

Figure 4   **Figure 5**

7. Fold waistband in half, right sides together, and sew end seams (Figure 5). Trim corners. Turn right side out. Hand-stitch folded edge of waistband in place.

8. Sew pocket squares with right sides together, leaving a 2-inch opening on one side. Trim corners. Turn right side out. Fold in seam allowance on opening and press.

9. Baste pocket to apron 4 inches from waistband and 8 inches from side. Topstitch close to side and bottom edges.

Flower

1. Fold and press fabric strip in half lengthwise, with wrong sides together. Use soluble marking pen to mark five flower templates (page 35) along the strip, starting and ending ½ inch from the short end, with the straight edge along the fold and leaving approximately ⅛ inch between stitching lines of each segment.

2. Using doubled thread, hand-stitch gathering stitches on pattern lines. When moving from one U to the next, go over the edge of the fabric fold and back into the pattern (Figure 6).

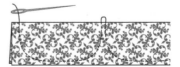

Figure 6

3. After each section is stitched, pull on the thread to gather the fabric into a petal. When all five petals are formed, knot the thread and then take a few stitches into the first petal to form a circular flower shape.

4. Glue a scrap of fleece or batting to the top of the shank button and trim around the edges. Cut a 2¼-inch-diameter circle from the skirt remnant and hand-sew gathering stitches around edge.

5. Place shank button fleece side down on wrong side of fabric circle and pull thread to gather fabric around the shank. Glue the covered button in the center of the flower.

6. Fold a small pleat in the base of a leaf and tack to hold. Repeat with a second leaf. Whipstitch or glue leaves to the back of the flower.

7. Sew a pin back to the back of the flower. Pin flower to apron pocket. ❖

Source: Blanc Et Noir fabric collection from Quilting Treasures.

Tips & Techniques

Machine-sew the flower by using a longer stitch length and adjusting tension. Sew as before, but don't backstitch at the beginning and leave long thread tails for gathering.

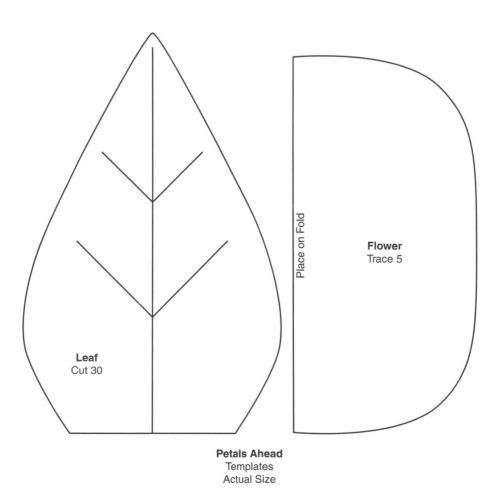

Leaf
Cut 30

Place on Fold

Flower
Trace 5

Petals Ahead
Templates
Actual Size

Apron Elegance

By Chris Malone

When it's time to dress up for a special occasion, you'll want to make an elegant apron in black and white with accents of red.

Finished Size
Adult small/medium

Finished Measurements
Length: 34 inches
Width at waist: 17 inches

Materials
- 44/45-inch-wide lightweight woven fabric:
    1⅛ yards white-with-black print
    ¼ yard black-with-white print (A)
    ¼ yard black-with-white print (B)
    ⅛ yard red-and-black print
- Scraps two additional black-with-white prints (C, D)
- Basic sewing supplies and equipment

Cutting
From white-with-black print:
- Cut one 41 x 28-inch rectangle for skirt.
- Cut one 40 x 5¾-inch strip for hem facing.

From black-with-white print (A):
- Cut two 3½ x 3½-inch squares for patchwork.
- Cut two 3½ x 3¾-inch rectangles for patchwork.
- Cut one 18 x 4½-inch strip for waistband.
- Cut one 3½ x 5½-inch rectangle for pocket.
- Cut one 5½ x 6½-inch rectangle for pocket lining.

From black-with-white print (B):
- Cut three 3½ x 3½-inch squares for patchwork.
- Cut two 4 x 30-inch strips for ties.

From scraps additional black-with-white prints (C, D):
- Cut three 3½ x 3½-inch squares from each for patchwork.

From red-and-black print:
- Cut two 1½ x 40-inch strips for skirt borders.
- Cut three 1½ x 5½-inch strips for pocket borders.

Assembly
Use ½-inch seam allowance unless otherwise indicated. Sew right sides together.

1. Arrange the 13 patchwork pieces in a row with the 3¾-inch (A) rectangles at each end. Using a ¼-inch seam allowance, sew together to make a 40 x 3½-inch strip. Press seams open.

2. Using a ¼-inch seam allowance, sew a red skirt border to the top and the bottom of the patchwork band. Press the seam toward the borders.

3. Press a ½-inch hem along both 28-inch sides of the skirt. Sew one long edge of patchwork to bottom of skirt. *Note: Do not open pressed side hems.* Press seam toward border.

4. Press a ⅜-inch hem along one long edge of the hem facing. With right sides together, pin unpressed side of facing to skirt bottom. Sew with a ½-inch seam allowance on the sides and a ¼-inch seam allowance along the bottom edge (Figure 1). Clip corners and turn facing right side out. Complete stitching side hems of skirt from the top of the facing to top edge.

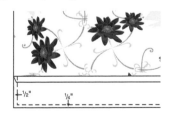

Figure 1

5. Pat facing flat and pin facing to the skirt. Turn skirt to the right side and stitch in the ditch to catch the top edge of the hem facing on the wrong side (Figure 2). Carefully remove pins before you sew over them.

Figure 2

6. Using a double row of basting threads, gather top edge of skirt to 17 inches. Adjust gathers evenly. Sew gathered edge of skirt to one long side of waistband, right sides together, leaving seam allowances extended on waistband (Figure 3). Press under ½ inch on opposite long edge of waistband.

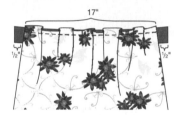

Figure 3

7. Fold each tie in half lengthwise with right sides together and sew down long edges and across one end. Trim corners and turn right side out. Press. Sew raw ends of ties to lower ends of waistband (Figure 4).

Figure 4

8. Fold waistband in half, right sides together, and sew short end seams (Figure 5). Trim corners and turn right side out. Slipstitch folded edge of waistband to the inside.

Figure 5

9. Using a ¼-inch seam allowance, sew a red pocket border to sides of pocket front. Press seams toward border. Sew remaining pocket border to bottom of pocket front. Press seam toward border (Figure 6).

Figure 6

10. Pin pocket front and lining together, right sides facing, and sew around all edges, leaving a 2-inch opening at bottom. Trim corners and turn right side out. Fold in seam allowance on opening and press.

11. Baste pocket to apron 4 inches from waistband and 8 inches from side. Topstitch pocket sides and bottom edges. ❖

Tips & Techniques

Quilters generally use a ¼-inch seam allowance to reduce bulk and save fabric—an important technique when working with tiny scraps. You'll find it equally helpful when piecing the patchwork and borders on this apron.

Granny Wrap

By Missy Shepler

Prairie points pretty-up a practical wrap apron!

Finished Size
Adult large

Finished Measurements
Length: 25½ inches
Width: 35½ inches

Materials
- 42-inch-wide lightweight woven fabric:
    1 yard print (A)
    1 yard print (B)
- 5-inch charm square package or ⅛ yard each 3 coordinating prints
- Basic sewing supplies and equipment

Cutting
From print (A):
- Cut one 36 x 28½-inch rectangle for apron front.

From print (B):
- Cut one 36 x 28½-inch rectangle for apron lining.
- Cut two 6½ x 7-inch rectangles for pocket.
- Cut three 2¼-inch strips the width of the fabric for apron tie.

From charm package or coordinating prints:
- Cut 20 (4 x 4-inch) squares for prairie points.

Prairie Points
1. Press each 4-inch square in half diagonally with wrong sides of fabric together (Figure 1).

Figure 1	Figure 2

2. With folded edge at bottom, fold triangle in half vertically and press (Figure 2).

Assembly
Use ¼-inch seam allowance unless otherwise indicated. Sew right sides together.

1. Sew ends of apron tie strips together on the bias. Trim seam allowance. Press seams open. Press under ¼ inch at each short edge. Press strip in half lengthwise with wrong sides together. Open strip and press raw edges to center crease. Fold strip in half again and press.

2. Place three prairie points on the right side of one pocket piece, aligning raw edges of points with the top 6½-inch edge of the pocket and having outside points ¼ inch from each pocket edge. Nest points inside each other to space evenly (Figure 3). Sew in place using a ⅛-inch seam allowance.

¼"

Figure 3

3. On wrong side of second pocket piece, draw a point, starting 2¼ inches from bottom edge at each side and ending ¼ inch above center bottom (Figure 4).

2¼"

Figure 4

4. Place pocket pieces right sides together with prairie points sandwiched between, aligning outer edges. Stitch around outer edge, following drawn triangular bottom line and leaving a 2-inch opening for turning. Trim seam allowance and clip corners. Turn pocket right side out. Press, turning seam allowance to inside at opening. Hand-stitch opening closed.

5. Pin pocket at an angle on apron front, 7 inches below top edge and 7½ inches from right side. Beginning ¼ to ½ inch from top edge of pocket/prairie-point seam, topstitch pocket to apron around side and bottom edges. Press prairie points and top ¼ to ½ inch of pocket down (Figure 5).

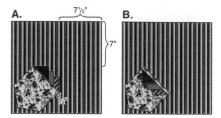

A.   7½"   B.

7"

Figure 5

6. Pin 17 prairie points along the right side of the apron front bottom edge, starting ¼ inch from side seam and ending ¼ inch from side seam with raw edges even. Nest prairies points as before. Stitch points to apron front using a ⅛-inch seam allowance.

7. Pin apron front and lining with right sides together along top and side edges. Smooth apron front over stitched prairie points. Pin bottom edges together. Stitch around outer edge of apron, leaving a 4- to 6-inch opening for turning on one side. Clip corners. Turn apron right side out. Press, turning under seam allowance on opening. Hand-stitch opening closed.

8. Center tie on apron front 4 inches below top edge. Pin. Stitch both edges of tie across width of apron, continuing stitching to ends of ties. ❖

Source: *Reminiscence fabric collection from Quilting Treasures.*

Holiday Hostess

By Missy Shepler

Showcase seasonal prints with this quick-to-stitch apron.

Finished Size
Adult medium/large

Finished Measurements
Approximately 30 to 34 inches, depending on yardage width. Apron is worn diagonally.

Materials
- 44/45-inch-wide lightweight woven fabric:
  1 yard each 2 coordinating holiday prints
- Basic sewing supplies and equipment

Cutting
From one holiday print:
- Fold yardage on a 45-degree angle. From extended single layer of fabric, cut three 2¼-inch strips the width of the fabric for ties.
- Square up remaining yardage. Cut largest square possible for lining.

From second holiday print:
- Cut one square the same size as lining.

Assembly
Use ¼-inch seam allowance unless otherwise indicated. Sew right sides together.

1. Sew short ends of apron tie strips together on the bias. Trim seam allowance. Press seams open. Press under ¼ inch at each short edge. Press strip in half lengthwise with wrong sides together. Open strip and press raw edges to center crease. Fold strip in half again and press.

2. With right sides together, sew apron front and lining together around outer edges, leaving a 6-inch opening for turning. Clip corners and turn apron right side out. Press.

3. Center tie on apron front 5½ inches above horizontal center of apron (Figure 1). Pin. Stitch both edges of tie across width of apron, continuing stitching to ends of ties.

Figure 1

4. To wear, fold top apron point down 3 inches above tie. Hold apron edges at ties and wrap apron around waist. Cross ties at back, then bring ties to center front waist and tie in a bow, allowing top of apron to ruffle (Figure 2a).

Figure 2a

If desired, pull top apron point up and tuck into tie or folded apron edge to form a temporary pocket (Figure 2b). ❖

Figure 2b

Source: *Holiday Traditions fabric collection from Hoffman California Fabrics.*

Very Berry

By Carolyn Vagts

Appliqué strawberries accent this tasteful apron that will keep you looking your "berry" best.

Finished Size
Adult large/extra-large

Finished Measurements
Apron skirt at waist: 24 inches
Apron bib: 11½ x 11½ inches
Overall length, excluding nonadjustable neck strap: 31 inches

Materials
- 44/45-inch-wide lightweight cotton fabric:
  2½ yards white print
  ⅝ yard red print
  Scraps red and green batik for appliqués
- No. 8 pearl cotton:
  green
  black
- ¼ yard lightweight paper-backed fusible web
- Scraps cut- or tear-away fabric stabilizer
- Basic sewing supplies and equipment

Cutting
From white print fabric:
- Cut one 48 x 40-inch rectangle for skirt.
- Cut two 9½ x 24¼-inch strips for pockets.
- Cut two 12 x 10-inch squares for bib.

From red print fabric:
- Cut two 5½ x 40-inch strips for waistband and ties.
- Cut two 2½ x 40-inch strips for binding.
- Cut one 3 x 40-inch strip for neck strap.
- Cut two 2½ x 12-inch rectangles for top of bib.

Appliqués
1. Fuse lightweight paper-backed web to scraps of red and green batik. Trace strawberry template (page 47) on paper side of web to make five appliqués, using red for strawberries and green for leaves and hulls.

2. Cut out on traced lines. Set aside.

Assembly
Use a ¼-inch seam allowance unless otherwise indicated.

1. Sew 2½-inch binding strips together on the diagonal, end to end, with right sides together (Figure 1). Trim seam allowance to ¼ inch and press seam open. Press binding strip in half lengthwise with wrong sides together matching raw edges.

Figure 1

2. Sew pocket pieces together so piece measures 9½ x 48 inches. Sew binding strip to right side of pocket strip with raw edges even (Figure 2). Fold binding to wrong side of the pocket and slipstitch in place.

Figure 2

3. Fold and press the pocket unit into quarters to help center placement of pocket appliqués. Remove paper backing from appliqués and fuse one strawberry appliqué to the center of each pocket center (Figure 3). Machine-stitch close to edges and add veins in leaves using straight stitch and matching threads.

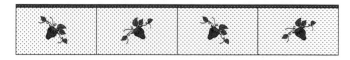

Figure 3

46

4. Using pearl cotton, backstitch vines with green; and stitch seeds on the strawberries with tiny black straight stitches.

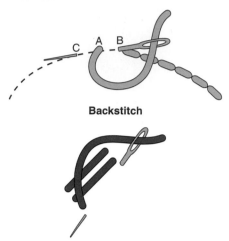

Backstitch

Straight Stitch

5. Center remaining strawberry appliqué horizontally on one bib rectangle, placing strawberry approximately 3¼ inches from top edge. Fuse and appliqué in place as for pockets.

6. Press the skirt rectangle in half with right sides together (Figure 4). Open up skirt rectangle. With right side up, draw a line across fabric ¼ inch above pressed line (Figure 5).

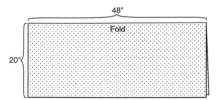

Figure 4

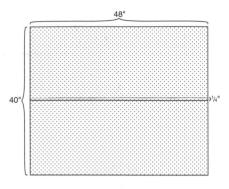

Figure 5

7. With right sides together, place pocket unit and apron skirt front together, aligning bottom edge of pocket unit with marked line (pocket body will rest on skirt lining). Sew across bottom edge of pocket unit on pressed fold line (Figure 6).

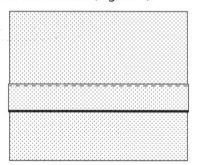

Figure 6

8. Fold skirt in half lengthwise with right sides together and sew both side seams. Turn right sides out and press. Sew along the three pocket lines to divide (Figure 7). Using a gathering stitch, sew across the top of the apron skirt and gather to approximately 24 inches.

Figure 7

9. With right sides together, sew a 2½ x 12-inch rectangle to the top edge of each bib rectangle. Press one seam up and one seam down.

10. Fold neck strap with right sides together and raw edges even. Sew long edge. Turn right side out and press with seam in center. Topstitch along both long edges.

11. Pin ends of neck strap to the front bib (Figure 8). Adjust length of strap, trim ends as needed, then repin in place. Pin bib lining on top of front, right sides together, with the length of the neck strap sandwiched between. Sew around the two sides and top. Turn right sides out and press. With linings together and raw edges even, center apron bib on apron skirt (Figure 9).

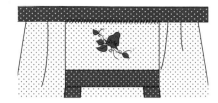

Figure 12

15. Turn ties right sides out and press. Hand-stitch opening closed across bib (Figure 12). Tack center top edge of waistband to bib. ❖

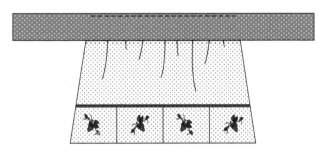

Figure 8

Figure 9

12. Sew the 5½-inch strips for waistband and ties together on the diagonal as for the binding strips. Fold in half lengthwise with wrong sides together and press. Cut 15 to 20 inches off one end to off-center the bias seam. Open back up.

13. Center strip, right sides together, along skirt edge, matching raw edges (Figure 10). Sew strip to skirt.

Very Berry
Template
Actual Size

Figure 10

14. Fold back into place with right side together. Starting at the apron skirt, sew to end of each tie (Figure 11).

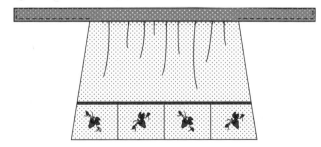

Figure 11

House of White Birches, Berne, Indiana 46711 DRGnetwork.com

See, Shop, Sew

Blank Quilting
(888) 442-5265
www.blankquilting.com

Hoffman California
Fabrics
(800) 547-0100
www.hoffmanfabrics.com

Moda Fabrics
(800) 527-9447
www.unitednotions.com

Oilcloth International
(323) 344-3967
www.oilcloth.com

Quilting Treasures
(800) 876-2756
www.quiltingtreasures.com

Designers

Janis Bullis
Pop-Over Smock, 11

Phyllis Dobbs
Sassy Pink Floral Apron, 14

Connie Kauffman
Chocolate Lover's Apron, 17

Chris Malone
Something to
  Crow About, 8
Petals Ahead, 32
Apron Elegance, 36

Janice Loewenthal
Gingerbread Men Apron, 24

Missy Shepler
Vintage Kitchen
  Cover-Up, 4
Handy Helper, 20
Granny Wrap, 39
Holiday Hostess, 42

Carolyn Vagts
Oilcloth Polka Dot, 28
Very Berry, 44

Metric Conversion Charts

Metric Conversions

yards	x	.9144	=	metres (m)
yards	x	91.44	=	centimetres (cm)
inches	x	2.54	=	centimetres (cm)
inches	x	25.40	=	millimetres (mm)
inches	x	.0254	=	metres (m)

centimetres	x	.3937	=	inches
metres	x	1.0936	=	yards

Standard Equivalents

⅛ inch	=	3.20 mm	=	0.32 cm
¼ inch	=	6.35 mm	=	0.635 cm
⅜ inch	=	9.50 mm	=	0.95 cm
½ inch	=	12.70 mm	=	1.27 cm
⅝ inch	=	15.90 mm	=	1.59 cm
¾ inch	=	19.10 mm	=	1.91 cm
⅞ inch	=	22.20 mm	=	2.22 cm
1 inch	=	25.40 mm	=	2.54 cm
⅛ yard	=	11.43 cm	=	0.11 m
¼ yard	=	22.86 cm	=	0.23 m
⅜ yard	=	34.29 cm	=	0.34 m
½ yard	=	45.72 cm	=	0.46 m
⅝ yard	=	57.15 cm	=	0.57 m
¾ yard	=	68.58 cm	=	0.69 m
⅞ yard	=	80.00 cm	=	0.80 m
1 yard	=	91.44 cm	=	0.91 m

1⅛ yard	=	102.87 cm	=	1.03 m
1¼ yard	=	114.30 cm	=	1.14 m
1⅜ yard	=	125.73 cm	=	1.26 m
1½ yard	=	137.16 cm	=	1.37 m
1⅝ yard	=	148.59 cm	=	1.49 m
1¾ yard	=	160.02 cm	=	1.60 m
1⅞ yard	=	171.44 cm	=	1.71 m
2 yards	=	182.88 cm	=	1.83 m
2⅛ yards	=	194.31 cm	=	1.94 m
2¼ yards	=	205.74 cm	=	2.06 m
2⅜ yards	=	217.17 cm	=	2.17 m
2½ yards	=	228.60 cm	=	2.29 m
2⅝ yards	=	240.03 cm	=	2.40 m
2¾ yards	=	251.46 cm	=	2.51 m
2⅞ yards	=	262.88 cm	=	2.63 m
3 yards	=	274.32 cm	=	2.74 m
3⅛ yards	=	285.75 cm	=	2.86 m
3¼ yards	=	297.18 cm	=	2.97 m
3⅜ yards	=	308.61 cm	=	3.09 m
3½ yards	=	320.04 cm	=	3.20 m
3⅝ yards	=	331.47 cm	=	3.31 m
3¾ yards	=	342.90 cm	=	3.43 m
3⅞ yards	=	354.32 cm	=	3.54 m
4 yards	=	365.76 cm	=	3.66 m
4⅛ yards	=	377.19 cm	=	3.77 m
4¼ yards	=	388.62 cm	=	3.89 m
4⅜ yards	=	400.05 cm	=	4.00 m
4½ yards	=	411.48 cm	=	4.11 m
4⅝ yards	=	422.91 cm	=	4.23 m
4¾ yards	=	434.34 cm	=	4.34 m
4⅞ yards	=	445.76 cm	=	4.46 m
5 yards	=	457.20 cm	=	4.57 m

E-mail: Customer_Service@whitebirches.com

HOUSE of
WHITE
BIRCHES
PUBLISHERS
SINCE 1947

The Best Apron Book Ever is published by DRG, 306 East Parr Road, Berne, IN 46711, telephone (260) 589-4000. Printed in USA. Copyright © 2009 DRG. All rights reserved. This publication may not be reproduced in part or in whole without written permission from the publisher.

RETAIL STORES: If you would like to carry this pattern book or any other DRG publications, call the Wholesale Department at Annie's Attic to set up a direct account: (903) 636-4303. Also, request a complete listing of publications available from DRG.

Every effort has been made to ensure that the instructions in this pattern book are complete and accurate. We cannot, however, take responsibility for human error, typographical mistakes or variations in individual work.

STAFF
Editor: Julie Johnson
Managing Editor: Dianne Schmidt
Technical Editor: Marla Freeman
Technical Artist: Nicole Gage
Copy Supervisor: Michelle Beck
Copy Editors: Angie Buckles,
  Amanda Ladig
Graphic Arts Supervisor:
  Ronda Bechinski

Graphic Artists: Glenda Chamberlain,
  Edith Teegarden
Art Director: Brad Snow
Assistant Art Director: Nick Pierce
Photography Supervisor:
  Tammy Christian
Photography: Matt Owen
Photo Stylist: Tammy Steiner

ISBN: 978-1-59217-243-6
2 3 4 5 6 7 8 9